By the same author

*War in Medieval Society* (1974)
*Borderland* (1984)
*Lightning Country* (1987)
*The King of Ashes* (1989)
*Clay* (1989)
*The Confirmation* (1992)
*Y Felan a Finnau* (1992)
*The City* (1993)
*Heroes* (1996)
*No Hiding Place* (1996)
*Abergavenny* (1997)
*The Wine Bird* (1998)
*Ice* (2001)
*At the Salt Hotel* (2003)
*Sea Lilies: Selected Poems 1984-2003* (2006)
*The Green Buoy* (2006)
*Trouble in Heaven* (2007)
*Tales of the Shopocracy* (2009)
*West Jutland Suite/Vestjysk Suite* (2009)
*The Forest Under the Sea* (2010)
*Fire Drill: Notes on the Twenty-First Century* (2010)
*A Year of Flowers* (2011)
*The Roaring Boys* (2012)
*Footfalls in the Silence* (2014)
*Wind Playing with a Man's Hat* (2016)
*Departure Lounge* (2018)
*Sherpas* (2018)
*Sunglasses* (2020)
*Afterlives* (2021)
*A Report to Alpha Centauri* (2021)
*Tsunami Days* (2023)

# Dunes of Cwm Rheidol

John Barnie

Published by Cinnamon Press
www.cinnamonpress.com



ISBN 978-1-78864-145-6

British Library Cataloguing in Publication Data. A CIP record for this book can be obtained from the British Library.



Designed and typeset in Bodoni by Cinnamon Press. Cover design by Adam Craig © Adam Craig .

Cinnamon Press is represented by Inpress

Acknowledgements

'Occupied' first appeared in *Planet*; 'Moss Covers the Trees' in *Poetry Wales*; and 'Mirror, Mirror' in *Red Poets*. 'Custard Apples' was published in Chinese as part of the Encyclopedic Poetry School's Shanghai Botanical Garden project.

# Contents

Say to them:
'Man has survived hitherto because he was too ignorant
to know how to realize his wishes. Now that he can realize
them, he must either change them or perish.'

William Carlos Williams, 'The Orchestra'

# Dunes of Cwm Rheidol

# Dunes of Cwm Rheidol

I'm going to the Sahel
where you see Wales is no refuge
but a statement of affairs
*compte rendu* for the past ten thousand years
      there's an auction in Cwm Rheidol
      'what will you give for this bullfinch, this green woodpecker?
      one worm-riddled fox?'
      the valley is clogged with cars from end to end
      can you make bread out of cars?
in the Sahel objects gravitate to the valleys of the mighty dunes
dig there for long forgotten bones even the bones of rivers
and riverine forests
dunes are restless in the Sahel
they must rush on having no roots no stiffening stalks
you might as well throw an anchor to anchor the wind
      I can hear them and see them
      the dunes of Cwm Rheidol
      slithering along the U-shaped valley
      to pile and rustle and swirl
      right where the auctioneer stood that day
      and nothing was bought.

# Roadkill

Travel on, that was the imperative
and we did down the narrow roads of Wales
Caernarfon, Dolgellau, Cemmaes, Machynlleth
macadam threaded through a needle's eye
sewing shrouds for the roadkill, a pheasant here a rabbit
there and I'm sure that was a raptor whose wing
flipped up in the slipstream of the car ahead
in a nonchalant goodbye
who could do justice to this in paint
I thought Goya but no, Bacon was the man
raw humans stripped of skin
writhing on the bed and not so different
from burst bodies on the roads
tubes of grey for intestines squeezed out fast
for Bacon was a hurried painter and we were hurried too
driving home or what we called home
he would pay attention to the squashed skull's eyes
pressed out of the sockets
just as if the *Screaming Pope* or the *Man in Blue*
lay down ahead in the road we travelled
because they were done for too.

# Solutions

Here's the temptation when winter tramples all over the earth
and birds grow leaner though you cannot see it under their feathers
and mice try to hide in your house and don't succeed
because you are there, much bigger and differentiated
with a brain to devise traps that snap over the neck or nose
or a live-trap where the mouse shivers, sweating its bodyweight

here's the temptation, as I say, to call on Mary
of the Renaissance-blue dress as if she were your mother
who could give comfort, take you to her unlike the gods
in their blokes' club issuing prohibitions, *noli* this and *noli* that
because wielding power is all gods ever have
like you returning to the house with the empty trap.

# Rivers

All rivers are great, even scampering streams
the puppies of the river world looked on by sombre
rocks and boulders, by mountains and fields
as little sparkling endless tails of something bounding
far out of sight; and from the height of the hills
I've seen the Usk on a grey day, slowworming
past the town, all its minutiae and small calculations
invisible from there, loach, bullheads and dace
suffered by the water with indifference; water
cannot speak of course, its talk is the bubbling
architecture of laughter without meaning, the mass
and shove of something giant, levees built and bridges
to get some edge, some control over this thing
that we need and can ride in our cockleshell skiffs
our wandering cargo ships, the dobbins we guide
safely to ports or not because rivers have treacheries
of their own, craftiness even like a crocodile's eyes
not seen until its jaws snap out your breath; yes
all rivers are great, even the scampering streams.

# Dead Swans on a Winter Coast

Patches of snow with orange beaks?
nature's never so outlandish, then it must be swans

a harsh winter's celebration of how things end
white keys of a crazy piano, boulders

for black keys that would be hard to play
I followed them as far as the peninsula's end

there was no one to grieve
so I walked beside them, taking it on.

# Had I Been There

Thinking of Katherine Mansfield
I wonder if there is any film of her
walking across the lawn of a summer garden
in clothes that look black or dark grey
but may have been red, tight-skirted
after the fashion with a little parasol
she pointed at the camera and waved
girl-like but not quite, with a skittish self-
conscious hand accentuated of course
by the jerkiness of the film, and beyond
a border of grey and white flowers
a Scotty dog yapping silently at the lens
could I have been there waiting to say
how dowdy and beautiful she looked
her hand already reaching up to draw
the curtain across a life she knew
would be brief which she had to fashion
into the poetry of the stories before
the flooding of her lungs with blood.

# What Should Be Done?

You say get rid of his books
he doesn't need that many now; but don't you see
books are his clothes
his house and the rooms of his mind
you want him to be happy in a care home's starvation camp
or at least silent, uncomplaining
because life is like that you say
passing from cloud to sunshine and back again
don't take away his roof
that book was an armchair favourite
you gave to the Charity
but charity can be a taking spider
retired ladies giving their time
thinking vaguely of all the refugees.

# Easy

There are few perquisites of old age
said the yellowhammer
except access to hospitals' dialysis machines
and open heart surgery, why
make such a toil of it, why let the days
creep by one another, the villainous stairs
you have to climb until you see far-off ungraspable hills

    whereas I perch in my yellow feathers at dawn
    always facing the sun.

# The Locals Were Puzzled

I've been thinking of Wordsworth's political persuasions
first he slept on the left then he slept on the right,
so, Mr Wordsworth, how was your night?

very good thank you, coming down to two boiled eggs
and buttered toast made by his women
the coal fire lit by the maid at 5; is there any correspondence today
no, so after the treat of being fussed over
it's greatcoat time for a walk round the lake

and there he goes, the angular poet-heron, a local feature
composing, so we supposed, each poem a silvery fish
to be swallowed whole down that lean gullet.

# Mrs Mountjoy

What happened to Mrs Mountjoy
club-footed and her unmarried daughter
making a go of it renting cold-water garrets
to students like me; darkness and cold
and I don't suppose her life got warmed
even by Mr Mountjoy whichever graveyard
he was in when I lived there, taking her foot
up and down the stairs to show penniless

rooms with curtains to draw for disappointment
across the night; a good place to freeze
which might have been Russian from what you read
all of us huddled in the skirting of life
getting up each day with a certain disbelief
that this is what there is and nothing better.

# The Years

All these books of years shelved in a library
I take one down to flick a dusty page or two,
that time in the outdoor swimming pool we played
knights-on-horses and I swam between a plump girl's legs
hoisting her up into the sun and air, squealing,
my horse stumbling toward an opponent whom she grappled
swaying till we fell with a splash into water
that uplifted us, sustained us, and I swear the hills

so familiar surrounding the town clapped their hands
can that be? the joy was never ours alone or so it seemed
but she is an old lady if still alive and the pool drained
bulldozed by the council not wanting more to do with it
I reach up, place the book back on its appointed shelf
the past is the past and I am not a great reader now.

# To the Editor

Poetry is a shark not a flatfish
whatever were you doing publishing flatfish?
we want thrashing about, blood

in the water, and you offer flatfish
throw them back into the dull heave
of ocean but look out for shark

finning itself in that eerie sinister
way around the hull of your magazine
no more flatfish, give us shark!

# Old Age on the Banks of the Usk

As if fishing in a backwater
children's squeals in a schoolyard far away
then the bell ringing them in

ample ripples catching the sky
as the river flows at speed but stays the same
until it's time and you can't deny

the sun slanting its rays, the air growing cold
creatures of the night creeping out, owls
ruffling feathers, swivelling their heads.

# You Don't See Them Now

A steamroller's industrial elephant patiently
flattening tarmac in our street, the driver
up there in a covered howdah with a flat cap
not a turban, spinning the wheel as the elephant

shuffled forward and back with the smell
of steam and oil, one of the world's marvels
and everything patient, the tarmac lorry
ready to slither more of the black shiny stuff

into the slow monster's way, easy now,
the round heavy rollers the machine-elephant's
feet obedient to the howdah-controller as
other workmen lean on shovels to watch.

# All Is Good

Your past is inscribed on clay tablets
in a script nobody else can read
or should I say shadowy paintings
in a cave never to be discovered

or a museum of forgotten things
the director sitting in his office
watching seasonal change in trees
glimpsed through dusty windows.

# Clearing up

What with plastic roses and the baby stirring
it was a well-timed event, the roses looked real
twined round the supports of the wedding pavilion
and better than real which only fade tarnishing the memory
far better artificial though sad when taken down
and put in boxes because there'll never be another

ah me, time sits in the shadow, there all along
sipping the day's prosecco sparkling in the sun
inspired to let things be for the happiness of an hour
a shared moment of which there are not so many
here on the rich and devastating Earth.

# Shacks

The body I thought was my house is just a shack
and good enough for many years, but now
the sills are rotting and you have to be careful of the steps
leading to a door that scrapes because its hinges have fallen;
oh well; all my family, I discovered, lived in shacks
and one by one I watched them totter and fall, what
must be a whole street if you placed them side by side;

is there any solution, something to stop age's worm;
none that I have found, so best to keep pressing on,
walk through woods in spring to admire the bluebells
and the wild garlic's refined culinary aroma; they
die off and rise again each year with no way to tell
one generation from the next; that's the way to go
not living in shacks where eventually the roof caves in.

# Good Times

All is forgettable in distress, everything
you thought you had ever been, even
love which can seem like a broken vase
nobody mourns for or the flowers that

once lolled and glowed above its rim;
too bad you say? life's charabanc has
moved on, raucous, down the road carrying
crates of beer, babycham for the ladies.

# What Was Revealed

He was pursued and looked round constantly
was it the wind, was it a distant train
     hope curled up in an alcove in the empty museum
     timidity scampered off on a thousand feet
at the station relatives gazed along rusted rails
you're all dead he shouted
if they heard there was no reply
what use is wraith talk
     the next part of the story involves
     a carriage shunted in a siding in 1941
     that is a different kind of silence
     not even a squeak of springs
     as someone shifts uneasily
     to wipe dirty panes with a sleeve
*where are you travelling to where is your ticket*
     he was ashamed life had been so poor
     he had never given it tenpence
     never reached in his pocket even for a twopenny bit.

# What the Poets Are Up To

Let's sit by the ornamental pond
where the liquid shimmering blue
enamel of a damsel fly quivers
where a water boatman skiffs itself
across the meniscus; isn't this
what poetry is for? and aquarium
goldfish palming themselves off
as the real thing; yes; yes? if not

listen to the crackle and explosion
of trees, explore the poisoned sand
along the shorelines of Earth.

II

# Occupied

*Beginning*

Twm said what do you mean barging in like this
and they shot him through the head
I screamed one threatened me with the butt of his gun
I collapsed on the floor, hands over my face
they left, someone an officer I think yelling at them
from an armoured vehicle in the street
who'd have thought it on Heol yr Eos
we're respectable here but that's all changed
they've got new rules and women can't go out alone
there's fear in every street, behind every door
poor Twm he didn't know what he was saying we
didn't know what occupation means, such times…

*Crossroads*

The clock keeps ticking but the clock goes wild
'they've erected a cross at the crossroads out of town'
whatever for, I said; we soon found out;
each dawn two are hanged one on each arm
it is a Scales of Justice but like one never seen;
they say the Mandrake grows under gallows
and if you dig it out be sure to plug your ears
against the shrill pierce of its scream as the root
is prized from the urine- and blood-drenched soil;
I don't know, could it be true; after curfew
you hear the mopeds as they cruise the streets
the driver and his pillion rider, automatics
slung across their shoulders weaving side to side,
sometimes a *rat-at* always in short bursts or
the distant explosion of a bomb, keep down
don't go near the window on this or any night.

*Bread and Parsnips*

There's queues for the Spar right round to Barclays
everyone with plastic bags, 'what did you get?' we ask,
'bread and parsnips' but when we reached the door
it was locked, the assistant inside mouthing 'n o t h i n g';
don't stand on corners don't look them in the eyes
scurry home like the tiny crabs we are glad still
to be crawling in the water of life but waiting for a hand
to part the seaweed curtain and pluck us out
to break us on the rocks to the harsh cries of the gulls.


*The Americans*

They have taken our radios, smashed our screens
mobile phones are the glitter of poison if found
'the Americans are coming to bomb us free'
accuracy guaranteed because of the technology,
there is nothing to fear from the Americans;
we peer anxiously at the pale luminescence of the sky;
the bombs came, Y Morlan, Great Darkgate Street
the Library, the University, bombed to rubble
and then the sky went silent, peerless, once again.


*Iridescence*

Search me if you like, you can't get past the truth
and the truth can't stop you falling; Cardiff's
gone and we don't know what happened to our friends
I feel I'm rolling a barrel of cats toward the river
miaowing and clawing determined to drown them
because what else is there to do, the safety net
so full of holes you couldn't catch a whale in it
since Twm left in an instant, in a flash, I knew,
I knew the days of iridescence were lost for ever.

*The Hospital*

Don't go to Bronglais, they took the drugs
raped the nurses, left the surgeons within a scalpel
of their lives, no need for packets of blood
they have their own splashed on walls
flowing in gutters, blood is blood is blood
they use it to place their mark on ruined homes,
the redwash of their trade, their mightiness,
if a tank points its nose at your front room
do not duck, no point in praying, search
your pockets, twopenny pieces will be enough
for a stranger to place them on your eyes.


*Heads*

Give it to me, give it to me the little girl said
I want it it's mine, it wasn't but I let her have it
and she went away sucking the crust of bread
they found the milkman in the abandoned quarry
and ten paces on they found his head
what do you make of that but in these days
nothing is to be made of a man found dead
and then the finding of his head, 'all shall be well
and all manner of things shall be well', whoever
said that had not been here, had never been au fait
with crossroads gallows, the weariness of it all.


*Testament*

There is no one on Pumlumon tonight only the stars shine down
Penrhyncoch is abandoned no news from the outlier towns
brick by brick, stone by stone, our lives have tumbled to the ground
this is an airless desert place, this is the valley of dry bones
concrete collapses a pack of cards shuffled for one more game
two pieces of wood can make a cross whereon to scratch a name
Twm was one of the first to die, to be tossed in a makeshift grave
the Americans came and bombed and nothing was left to save.

# Expendable

Everyone in the tank regiment was dead
and major rust had taken over the field
you can depend on rust to finish the job

'the world will never be the same'—but it is
Mary, Joseph and Jesus trudging through snow
while the tanks, our backbones, rust in the night.

# What I Heard

If you can't feed on human misery asked the crows
what can you feed on?
and continued pecking the eyes of the dead soldiers
human crows at the border asked the same thing
pecked at the women crossing

drank till the moon became dizzy
considered extending their tattoos
on arms that had hands that were extensions of their minds
eyeing the women who were the sorrowful extensions
of human-kind.

# Silence is Best

That's one of the complications of language, the general said,
that I can give orders for atrocities in Japanese
and you can hang me in English
and you can commit atrocities in English and nobody
hangs you because you won; is any language guilt-free?

words creep on the page, are stuffed in dictionaries
like nits in the hair in a prison camp
and no mother to lean you over a table
lovingly combing them out on old newspaper
with its dated report of the latest executions.

# Mirror, Mirror

Salt of the Earth, that's the British
and they still haven't given up their
civilising mission; what would you expect

from the foremost white men ever
to have lived; did you see that photo
of a soldier saving an Afghan girl

it tells you everything; dawn cracks open
its blazing eye and it's amazing how
it dwarfs the smouldering compounds.

# Observant

They're dying after a brief introduction to life
the general said surveying youth torn
on the autumn battlefield; he was a botanist of sorts

    and had noted two rarities
    among the severed limbs and heads
    the tiniest flowers only an expert would know
    or think exceptional in any way

stretcher bearers tramped all over the chaos
the flowers were lost in the mud
they'll rise again, the general said, next Spring.

# M.A.D.: The Sequel

The President at first demurred
then concurred
power makes the keenest mind
blurred
logic a tonic to be drunk on its own
     the generals put on their best fatigues
     no one could ever be in their league
cities vanished like popcorn popping
the band started playing
the generals danced
neither courtly nor elegant hand in hand
in the bunker of Joint Command
the look in their eyes showed no surprise
bombs had become their own sunrise
     birds stopped singing
     lives burnt in a flash
     cry if you must
     there was no one to gather
     the heart's dust.

# Address to the Bricklayers

Bricklayers! set aside your hods
lay down your trowels
for the now it is war and the tinkle of bricks
as buildings collapse
    you are not needed
    but you will be needed
    when brickworks operate again
    when the crying is over
    the deceased deposited as gifts to the earth
load your hods, climb the scaffolding
see how high you can go
to the rhythmic churning of cement-mixers
    let me hear you raise a cheer
    out of death comes life
    out of suffering renewal
    and you will be there to see it
    be attentive
    go about your business
that is all.

III

# Encounter

Hello, what's this battlefield bravado
of bijoux tanks spread across the hillslope's
soft-fall detritus meaning twigs, oak leaves
crumbled bits of bracken, and stones
to clamber across for a good view before
careering forward with a dip and stumble
the battle for life ongoing not stopping
beneath a canopy of leaves, in winter
a canopy of twigs, outer-uppermost
reaches of the universe for black beetles
on the Rholben, and what of that, isn't
reality negotiable and dependent on…
I couldn't say but have to get down
to address this tank's design flaw which is
up-and-tumble-rolled on their backs, legs
suddenly useful only for semaphoring,
armoured carapace death-trapped—*Help*
though no help at hand except a clumsy
lumberer who kneels and with a finger
gently pokes the tank to rights; no thanks
because this is evolution and our paths
swerve away from each other, the human
returning to the busy town, the beetle
bulldozing, barging, trundling on as best
it can; how many upend, never to be saved
dying with a wave of traction devices.

# In the Golden Stubbled Field

I watched harvesters stacking wheat in sun-coloured stooks
it was a Black Mountains summer's day and I the only one there
watching from the lane this Brueghel festival occasion until

there was one square left standing in the middle of the field
around which they gathered, men and women, two dogs with lolling
tongues, expectation stilling the sun for just that moment

when a frightened rabbit bolted out and the dogs set off and chased
and one man threw a cudgel that rolled end over end in slow
motion or so it seemed to me watching from the lane.

# At the Station

A porter has a basketful of pigeons which at the appropriate time
he releases, checking his fob watch
and up they go with a clap of wings

circling as if for strength or even to refuse
the long flight ahead of them to nothing but a hutch
in some Valleys town.

# Moss Covers the Trees

Reap what you sow, a harsh command
the boat-shaped coffin ready for all, knocking
against the harbour wall of the church or chapel of rest
though rest may be something no longer found
'doctor, give me something to take off reality'
the surgeries are closed, didn't you know
and birds of paradise have scarpered to the last few trees
to die in radiance; plough the land, sow the seed
wait through the dull parish of winter to see
what comes up, take the tares with the wheat
tares may be tasty when with bent backs under a driving sky
we harvest what we can; we sowed and we sowed
what more do you want from us, meaning God
whose airwaves are choked with static
something must be wrong even in heaven
that ill-at-ease mansion too big for the occupants
I heard the father, son, and Mary had packed up and gone
leaving the holy ghost to spook the rooms
hollow and empty for all our prayers.

# 2084

We tried crying in the dark
laughing at the Sun, nothing worked
*bang-bang* riveting the iron
of the ship we sailed in full knowledge
onto the rocks; there was a squawk
of seabirds lifting out of the way
of the petrochemical spills though
sandworms and crawlers were
not so lucky; survivors reached
the edge of the megacity to enter
the timeless ruin of our world.

# The Memorial Committee Makes a Decision

Why not continue to sing and dance
why not let musical instruments pile
in deserted forests to be our monument

it could merely be the clack of spoons
nothing more, mouth harp, banjo twang
or tubas and flutes, simple or complex

bring them out, add them to the heap
'see, this is what we were' a message left
not in hope as rust and worms will

decide on that, but a jumbled cairn
glorious just to have been here, fine
to have said 'we were capable of joy'.

# Violence as Psychotherapy

All I remember about Goldschmidt's life
was the assault on his house
people as wasps but worse than wasps
which don't hate you but are the attack
machines of the wild green earth

people are steamier, have the viciousness
of minds gone wrong when they think they are right
climaxing with a blow to the head
hurt of the object being the release
needed to express their normality again.

## Global

Was anything left alive?
I wouldn't go to the bees to ask that
nor to the choughs who sailed down the cliffs at your approach

    and how to ask it anyway?
    in the cracked approaches of verse
    as if with a votive offering at the ruined temple?
    come on, you know better than that

you know how the faces of humans pressed against life's windows
ducked to parry the blows they had struck against themselves

    in the late days there was a crackling in the air
    the sands of the rustling deserts a sibilation
    whispering something you did not wish to hear.

# Reveille

There's a lot I don't understand
in my ape-like mechanical way
ships that sail at dawn laden with regrets
past quays where junked computers
wait to be picked apart for rare metals
by the urban poor in China; Earth
is a mouth and we its teeth; here am I
safe for the now as it seems though
another dawn is surprised to find me
emerging out of darkness still alive.

# Looking for His Teeth

Where are his teeth? I heard
Koobi Fora, I heard the Sahel
I heard a gravel pit in Wiltshire
we have the jawbone and carry it in cloth
touch it with white cotton gloves
did he lose them in time's long slow trudge across the Earth
was he careless
     some things are easy to lose, money, keys
     stone tools, though these were mostly cast-offs
     new ones simple to make
     but teeth are carried in the mouth's wet cave
     they are useful
     I wouldn't be without mine, would you?
it's a hands-and-knees job searching for teeth
while the Sun hammers the Earth without regard
     the Sun our enemy
     also our friend.

# Be Honest

The poet owns nothing; do you say you own poems?
deceit, even though the book carries your name
perhaps has a photograph like a well-forged passport
the reader turns over in the shop, so good in fact

it passes the scan at the desk; nonetheless fake
because poems ride in on winter storms, are sudden
illuminations when the sun lights up the hills and
what can you honestly say you had to do with that?

# Rereading *Almayer's Folly*

In those days there were what I call paragraphs
pages long, like diving and seeing how far you can swim
underwater holding your breath; somewhere up above
there is sparkling sun breaking and refracting on the uneven surface,
you might even be called, who knows, about something important
but the paragraph goes on and on at the turn of pages, great
walls of it, each word trowelled in by a master craftsman,
who would build such walls now, who would dare, leaving
them abandoned in tropical forests for the explorative reader
to smash through and clear the tangle of vines and roots,
here was a man who knew about paragraphs of worth
lasting under starry nights and sunshine-driven showers of rain,
close the book, others will come and find them again.

# Solo

Death has a way of planting black flags
and not just for us, any buzzard or rabbit
will do as he goes about the world stooping
here and there, the Earth's sexton alert

to perquisites of a job he has had
for three billion years; think about that;
and all that time he found no mate
to come home to, tramping deserts

searching the poles; if he had wings
and could fly away to Venus perhaps
or Mars, but what would he do there, or
on the Moon's regolith shuffling dust;

Death would like to be a card player
saying 'spades are trumps', brandishing
the ace, but no one is there to see his

    astonishing good luck.

# Player-Piano

The daycentre player-piano tinkles
'Heaven is Waiting', good enough to tap to
on the arm of an upholstered chair;
as suddenly, it stops with a fit of sulks

its talents made for something mighty
like a hotel lobby with fashionable guests
checking in and bags being trolleyed
by waistcoated flunkies to the lifts.

# Antiques

I almost bought today a Roman key
second century, but where's the lock
and what would be behind the door
the past's I.O.U. perhaps reckoning
the first laugh's as good as the last
a cupboard of skeletons tumbling
out because they can't keep the joke
secret any longer, such a rattle of grins.

# The Way To Do It

It was only a fragment but what does that matter
the last known work by the great master
who passed his days like the rest of us
filling in time with brushes and paint
as a bricklayer does with mortar and trowel
both had the same satisfaction
faced the same hurricane over the flatlands of life
neither said goodbye
that fussy tidying up of the edges which only happens in books
the one had a pompous funeral
the other a shuffle of widow and mates
let them down easy Mister Undertaker
and on the return let the drummer bang his drum
let the trumpeter outsparkle the sun.

# Return to Sender

Looking through my address book I find it a cemetery
there are many monumental names
it is hard-hard to unwind friends from their repose

enemies lie here too but forgiven
under the blank face of their undoing
as I hope they forgave me; there's no help for it

time is hauled on a wooden cart flinging oblivion
on vast crowds, including those who hanged themselves
running with open arms into the grave.

# Old Man Dozing

How easy it is to sag in an easy chair
letting the brain waves, if that is what they are,
slowly wash over pebbles as it might be

an island in the Baltic Sea where brackish
water is the air for small marine plants swaying
like hula girls, Pacific or Baltic who cares

detail is nothing, let time lapse and swing
green as the orchard you once dreamed
of lying out in, tucked up under a crochet'd

counterpane, the sun going down, still
sparkling through leaves, while your parents
are not far away, and you are never alone.

# Problems with Punctuation

'He ate his last egg and Death said "time now"'
or should that be 'time, now'; 'ah'
the creative writing tutor intervened, 'the eternal
battle with the comma, I've danced
the hokey-cokey with it all my life
and who knows in the end if you get it right';

the comma such an insignificant scratch
pattering across pages, humility on the go,
shouldered aside by its brothers and sisters
until 'that's it, it's over', the full stop insists.

## On the Tiles

'He polished his teeth with Vim' well you've got to haven't you
if you want a good night out, the moon a piece of lemon rind
floating over the city's lights, red buses following their routes

bars filling with a flummery of noise, shop windows luminous
with mannequins and jewels, you've got to have that bright smile
of the lion or leopard ready for any victim that offers a bite

hmm, ramm, into his neck so the evening can be showered
with roman candles before returning to a crumpled room with
enough of the past to prepare you for weeks of desolation.

# Cheers

Pass the port or the whisky or the wine
whichever you prefer to douse the fire
of humanity's passage over the Earth

     so different from the thrush or the blackbird
     who turn green handles on a green door

while we play at being masters of it all
masking the stars with a display of lights
under which we plunder and rob ourselves.

# Have You Seen Him, Too?

I am haunted by that old man 'Mother Earth, let me in!'
is that all he can say after so many years, all he can think of?

the earth unresponding, though the world reels him back
to the comfort of a floral carpet, easy chair, kiddy's beaker

'how are you feeling now? *a l l   r a i g h t ?*' no he's not
he wants that stick he tapped with night and day

certain there is a door, 'Mother Earth, Mother Earth

    let me in.'

# Conscience

You were remiss there, platform ticket in hand
passing the barrier to the old life while
what you did steamed away

the past cannot be so easily delivered into the past;
the face at the window pale as the moon
ahead of you on the concrete lane.

# Silverbristles

Here comes Old Silverbristles
he never thought of that when he was eighteen
and his hair was black
how long does hair take to rot in the grave
he doesn't know
and anyway burning's best
when it goes up with a whump
Silverbristles reads a lot
he looks about at features of the Earth
haphazard items like himself
hears the collared doves starting up at dawn
life is short and days are the flicker-books
he had as a child of, was it, a dancing lady
or a running horse flickflickflick
and the lady danced and the horse ran
almost everything discarded now
so though he owns many things
he is naked and alone.

# Custard Apples

Some day I'll travel to the land
where custard apples grow, reach up
and pluck one among leaves and the sun's
glittery steel, holding its plumpness
weighing it gently; it will be autumn
but the tree will renew its leaves
a perpetual machine for greenness

because this is the tropics where
everything lives to a full intensity
unlike where I live and autumn
brings on winter, the giving up
and shrivelling of life to a memory;
I will cut open the silk of its purse
to reveal the creamy pale flesh

the black diamonds of its seeds
savouring the sweet custard taste;
I am past life's autumn now, winter
before the windows of my eyes
telling me it is time, but let there be
such moments yet, let there be
ebony seeds to scatter for a while.

Milton Keynes UK
Ingram Content Group UK Ltd.
UKHW010834240823
427277UK00004B/60